FEBRUARY

A MONTH OF REPRODUCIBLES AT YOUR FINGERTIPS!

Grades 2–3

Editor:
Darcy Brown

Writers:
Darcy Brown, Susan Hohbach Walker

Art Coordinator:
Clevell Harris

Artists:
Clevell Harris,
Mary Lester, Rob Mayworth, Kimberly Richard,
Barry Slate, Donna K. Teal

Cover Artist:
Jennifer Tipton Bennett

T0204574

©1998 by THE EDUCATION CENTER, INC.
All rights reserved except as here noted.
ISBN #1-56234-230-4

Manufactured in the United States
10 9 8 7 6 5 4 3 2 1

Table Of Contents

February Free-Time

Monday	Tuesday	Wednesday	Thursday	Friday
Recognize the importance of a healthy heart during American Heart Month. Exercise your heart today with activities like running, jumping rope, or playing basketball. 	Read about the Groundhog Day legend. Will it be an early spring, or do you expect six more weeks of winter? 	Elizabeth Blackwell's birthdate is February 3, 1821. She was the first woman to become a medical doctor. Write a list of jobs you would like to have as an adult.	February 5 is Weatherperson's Day. Write a weather forecast for your town.  "Today it will be sunny."	Pay-A-Compliment Day© is February 6. Pay a compliment to five different people today.  "You're a very good listener."
Laura Ingalls Wilder, author of the *Little House* books, was born on February 7, 1867. Can you name some of the characters in her stories? "Little House"	Happy birthday, Abraham Lincoln! This president was born on February 12, 1809, in Kentucky. Ask other students to name the states where they were born.	This country's first magazine, *The American Magazine*, was published on February 13, 1741. List five of your favorite magazines. 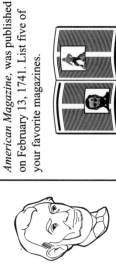	Don't let February 14 pass without making a Valentine's Day card for a special friend or family member. "Be Mine"	Ferris Wheel Day is held on the birthdate of its inventor, George Washington Gale Ferris. In a paragraph, write how it feels to be riding on a Ferris wheel. 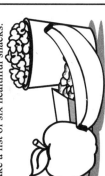
Presidents' Day falls on the third Monday. We celebrate the birthdays of George Washington and Abraham Lincoln. How many other U.S. presidents can you name?	Celebrate National Cherry Month by writing a recipe for a new snack made with cherries. 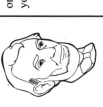	February is Potato Lovers Month. List all the ways you know how to eat potatoes.	Student Volunteer Day—February 20—brings attention to students who volunteer in schools or communities. Have you ever volunteered? How did it make you feel? "I'd like to help."	February is National Music Month. Name five of your favorite artists.
George Washington was born on February 22, 1732. How old would he be if he were alive today?	February marks Responsible Pet Owner Month. List responsible ways to take care of pets. "Fido" 	Homes For Birds Week is celebrated annually, the third week in February. Design a bird feeder for the birds around your school. 	February is Snack Food Month. Make a list of six healthful snacks.	Leap year gives February a 29th day every four years. Write a story that tells how you would feel if you had a birthday every four years. **29**

Note To The Teacher: Have each student staple a copy of this page inside a file folder. Direct students to store their completed work in their folders.

3

February
Events And Activities For The Family

Directions: Select at least one activity below to complete as a family by the end of February.
(Challenge: See if your family can complete all three activities.)

National Children's Dental Health Month

In observance of National Children's Dental Health Month, have your family brush up on their dental hygiene. Have each family member keep a chart for one week to track the number of times he brushes and flosses his teeth, and eats healthful snacks. At the week's end, have each family member evaluate his chart. Reward good dental hygiene with a healthful snack like apple wedges, cheese and crackers, or carrot slices.

George Washington's Birthday

February 22 marks the observance of George Washington's birthday. After retelling your favorite version of George Washington and the cherry tree, have your family prepare this delicious cherry crisp. Follow the recipe to make the crisp. By George! This crisp is incredible!

Cherry Crisp
(serves 6–8)

1 can cherry pie filling
1/2 cup packed brown sugar
1/4 cup flour
1/4 cup oatmeal
3 tablespoons softened butter

Preheat oven to 350°. Pour the cherry pie filling into a greased loaf pan. Mix the remaining ingredients together until crumbly; then pour the mixture over the cherries. Bake 30–35 minutes, or until the topping is golden brown. Serve warm.

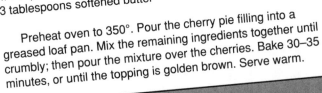

Read To Your Child Day

What better way to show children you love them than by reading to them! Read To Your Child Day is celebrated annually on February 14. Foster reading development by reading aloud *every* day! Some excellent read-aloud choices are:

- *Amazing Grace* by Mary Hoffman (Dial Books For Young Readers, 1991)
- *Henry And Mudge* series by Cynthia Rylant (Simon & Schuster Children's Division)
- *A House Is A House For Me* by Mary Ann Hoberman (Puffin Books, 1982)
- *Justin And The Best Biscuits In The World* by Mildred Pitts Walter (Lothrop, Lee & Shepard Books; 1986)
- *Junie B. Jones* series by Barbara Park (Random House Books For Young Readers)
- *The New Kid On The Block* poems by Jack Prelutsky (Greenwillow Books, 1984)
- *Secret Place* by Eve Bunting (Clarion Books, 1996)
- *Stuart Little* by E. B. White (HarperCollins Publishers, Inc.; 1990)

Note To The Teacher: Distribute one copy of this reproducible to each student at the beginning of the month. Encourage each family to complete at least one activity by the end of February.

GROUNDHOG DAY

Groundhog Day is a custom based on ancient and traditional weather signs. On February 2 the groundhog emerges from its burrow. If the groundhog sees its shadow, it gets scared back into its den and there will be six more weeks of winter. But if the groundhog does not see its shadow, spring will soon come.

Shadow Shenanigans

Your students will go hog-wild with these shadow shenanigans! On a sunny morning, take your class outside and explain how the sun's rays create long and short shadows, depending on how high the sun is up in the sky. Then have pairs of students conduct this easy experiment. Have one student stand on the sidewalk with his back to the sun. His partner then draws a chalk outline of the shadow made on the sidewalk; then he writes his partner's name next to the outline. Have partners switch places and repeat the chalk drawing process. Later that same day, take your students back outside to the same location to conduct their experiments again. Have students compare their morning shadows with their afternoon shadows. For an additional activity, challenge each pair of students to measure the length of their shadows in inches and centimeters.

Punxsutawney Phil

Every year Punxsutawney Phil emerges from his burrow on February 2 to make his annual weather prediction. Display a U.S. map in a prominent location. Explain to your students that Punxsutawney is a town in Pennsylvania. Select a student to find this state and town on the map. Then have another youngster locate *your* school's state and town on the map. Have students calculate the approximate distance from their school to Punxsutawney, Pennsylvania.

What's The Weather?

Well, that all depends on the groundhog! Share a weather forecast from a local newspaper or television broadcast. Also involve students in a discussion about some of the weather words from the box. Then duplicate one copy of page 8 for each student. Have each student write a weather report for Gertie Groundhog using some of the weather words. If desired set up a weather studio in your classroom. Invite each student to read his weather report to his classmates. What's the weather? Sunny with a chance for some fun!

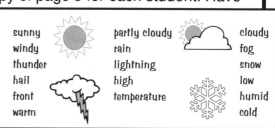

sunny	partly cloudy	cloudy
windy	rain	fog
thunder	lightning	snow
hail	high	low
front	temperature	humid
warm		cold

Name_____

Searching For Shadows

Use the numbers on the suns and clouds to complete the facts.
Color each sun or cloud as you use its number.

Row A

```
   7        □        □        2        □        8
x □      x 6      x 1      x □      x 3      x □
-----    -----    -----    -----    -----    -----
   7        0        3        6       15       16
```

Row B

```
   □        8        7        9        □        □
 x 4      x □      x □      x □      x 4      x 1
-----    -----    -----    -----    -----    -----
  12       40       14       36       20        3
```

Row C

```
   9        □        5        □        6        □
 x □      x 5      x □      x 8      x □      x 3
-----    -----    -----    -----    -----    -----
  27       25       10        8       12        9
```

Row D

```
   □        □        7        □        4        9
 x 7      x 7      x □      x 9      x □      x □
-----    -----    -----    -----    -----    -----
  35       28       21       18        8       45
```

Row E

```
   □        3                          6        □
 x 4      x □                        x □      x 2
-----    -----                      -----    -----
  16       12                         24        0
```

Bonus Box: Can you write <u>nine</u> different multiplication fact problems using only the factors 3, 4, and 5? Show your work on the back of this paper. Be sure to answer each fact, too!

Groundhog Facts And Opinions

Read each sentence.
Color the sun if the sentence is a *fact*.
Color the cloud if the sentence is an *opinion*.

1. Another name for a groundhog is a *woodchuck*.

2. All groundhogs have scary shadows.

3. Groundhogs live in burrows or dens under the ground.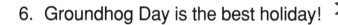

4. Groundhogs hibernate in winter.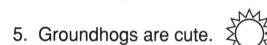

5. Groundhogs are cute.

6. Groundhog Day is the best holiday!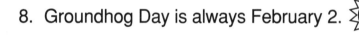

7. Groundhogs eat plants like alfalfa and clover.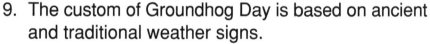

8. Groundhog Day is always February 2.

9. The custom of Groundhog Day is based on ancient and traditional weather signs.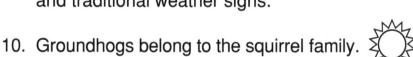

10. Groundhogs belong to the squirrel family.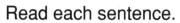

Bonus Box: On the back of this sheet, draw a picture of what you think a groundhog might have been dreaming about all winter.

What's The Weather?

Help Gertie Groundhog write a weather report on the lines below.

VALENTINE'S DAY

Valentine's Day can be traced to a variety of sources—the ancient Roman festival called *Lupercalia,* the old English belief that birds choose their mates on February 14, and one or more saints in the early Christian church named Valentine. Many people observe this day by sending gifts of flowers, candy, or cards called *valentines* to their loved ones.

Lovely Letters

Turn your youngsters on to letter writing with this lovely idea! Duplicate one copy of the letter pattern on page 13 and one copy of the envelope pattern on page 14 for each student. Then have each youngster write a friendly letter to Cupid. To create an envelope, have each child write the mailing and return addresses on his envelope pattern. Then instruct him to cut out the shape along the bold lines, fold the cutout in half, and glue or tape the sides of the envelope to form a pocket. Have students fold their letters and slip them inside their envelopes. If desired, display the envelopes on a bulletin board titled "Lovely Letters." Now that's a very special delivery!

Heart Matters

Get to the heart of Valentine's Day when your students make cards for secret valentines. Tell your students that one of the oldest Valentine's Day customs consisted of a man drawing a woman's name from a jar. The selected woman became the man's valentine. Direct each youngster to write his name on a slip of paper. Collect the slips and place them in a jar. Have each student, in turn, draw a slip from the jar. The name the student selects becomes his secret valentine friend. Have the student make a heart-shaped card for his special valentine. Collect the cards and redistribute them to the named students. At the end of the day, invite your youngsters to reveal themselves to their valentine friends.

Rockin' Valentines

Review basic math facts with this rockin' version of musical chairs. Cut out and laminate a class supply of red construction-paper hearts. Write a different addition or subtraction fact on each cutout. Next divide students into two groups; then arrange an equal number of student chairs back-to-back for each group. Place one heart facedown on each chair. To play the game, have each student stand in front of a different chair. Instruct the students to walk around the chairs while music is playing. When the music stops, have each student flip over a heart and solve the problem. The student with the highest sum (or difference) is out. Continue play until only one child in each group is left. Reward the winning youngsters with a sticker or other small treat. Then reprogram the hearts and play the game again!

Cupid's Collection Of Contractions

Write the contraction for each word pair on the line.

Remember that when two words are written together as a contraction, you use an apostrophe to show where letters have been left out.

1. are not	2. I am	3. you have	4. you are
aren't			

5. it will	6. they have	7. we are	8. he would

9. had not	10. I would	11. does not	12. she will

13. you will	14. they would	15. let us	16. would not

Bonus Box: On the back of this sheet, write a valentine story that includes five contractions.

Name_____

Valentine Delivery

Write the words in ABC order on the envelopes in each column.

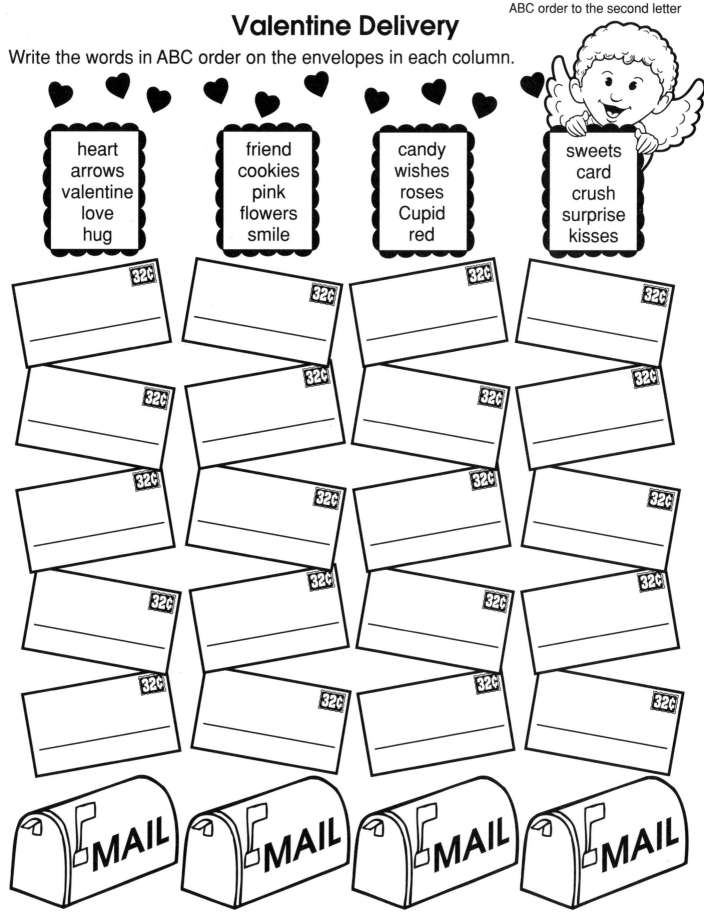

heart	friend	candy	sweets
arrows	cookies	wishes	card
valentine	pink	roses	crush
love	flowers	Cupid	surprise
hug	smile	red	kisses

MAIL   MAIL   MAIL   MAIL

Sweet Treats

Color the coins needed to buy each piece of candy.

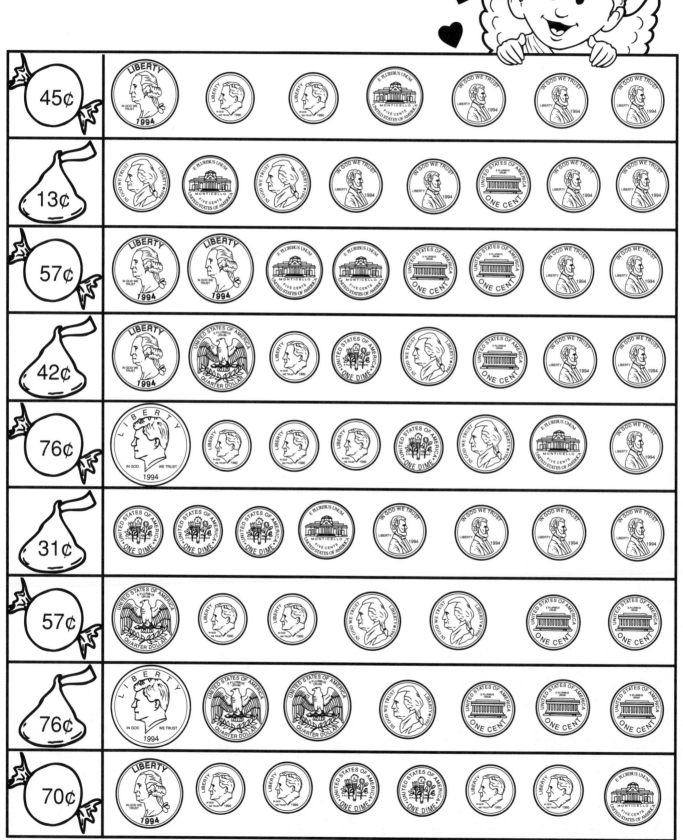

©1998 The Education Center, Inc. • *February Monthly Reproducibles* • Grades 2–3 • TEC941 • Key p. 63

Note To The Teacher: Use with "Lovely Letters" on page 9.

Note To The Teacher: Use with "Lovely Letters" on page 9.

Name _____

Hearty Plurals

Read each word.
Write its plural on the line.
Color the hearts using the code.

cherry

cookie

heart

candy

kiss

rose

wish

card

hug

box

arrow

crush

Color Code
Add *s* = red
Add *es* = pink
Change *y* to *i* and
   add *es* = purple

Fall In Love With A Book!

Put Your ♥ Into Reading!

Find A New Adventure In A Book!

I Love To Read!

Note To The Teacher: Duplicate the bookmarks on construction paper, cut them out, and distribute them to your students.

BLACK HISTORY MONTH

Invite your youngsters to explore the history and heritage of Black Americans with this unique collection of activities and reproducibles.

A Wealth Of Information

Begin your unit by sharing this information about some famous Americans with your students:

- **Rosa Lee Parks** was born in Tuskegee, Alabama, in 1913. She attended the Alabama State Teachers College. In 1943 Rosa became one of the first women to join the National Association for the Advancement of Colored People (NAACP). She was arrested in a 1955 boycott of the Montgomery, Alabama, bus system when she refused to give up her seat to a white person.

- **Elijah McCoy** was born in Colchester, Ontario, in 1843. His parents were slaves who had fled to Canada from Kentucky. Elijah was a famous inventor. Some of his inventions include a lubricator for steam engines, an ironing table, a lawn sprinkler design, and a drip cup.

- **Harriet Tubman** was born a slave in Bucktown, Maryland, in 1820. In 1849 Harriet escaped from slavery and fled to Philadelphia. During the 1850s she helped more than 300 slaves escape to freedom on the Underground Railroad.

- **Booker T. Washington** was one of the most important black leaders of his time. He attended the Hampton Institute in Virginia to become a teacher. In 1881 he founded the Tuskegee Institute—a school for Black Americans.

- **Shirley Chisholm**, born in Brooklyn, New York, in 1924, became the first black woman to serve in the United States Congress in Washington, D.C. She worked hard to meet the needs of American citizens.

- **George Washington Carver** was a scientist who discovered more than 300 uses for peanuts. Born a slave in Diamond, Missouri, he worked to pursue a career in agriculture at Iowa State Agricultural College. In 1896 Carver became a teacher at the Tuskegee Institute.

- **Michael Jordan** was born in Brooklyn, New York, in 1963. He grew up in Wilmington, North Carolina, and attended the University of North Carolina at Chapel Hill. Michael plays basketball for the Chicago Bulls. In 1994 he took time off to play baseball for the Chicago White Sox. Michael is 6 feet 6 inches tall!

- **Louis Armstrong** was a famous jazz musician. He played the cornet and the trumpet during the 1920s and early 1930s. Louis played with bands and was often a soloist. He liked to sing, too. Two of his most famous songs include "Hello Dolly" (1963) and "What A Wonderful World" (1968).

Marvelous Mobiles

After sharing the facts above, invite your youngsters to make these marvelous mobiles! Duplicate pages 19, 20, and 21 for each student. Have each youngster cut out his photo cards and his fact cards. Instruct him to match each photo card to its fact card; then have him lay the pairs on his desk. Next direct each youngster to color his picture cards, cut them out, and match each one to its corresponding pair. To make a mobile, have each student tape a 14-inch length of yarn to the back of each set of cards as shown. Next have him decorate a 3" x 20" strip of tagboard as desired; then direct him to equally tape each length of yarn to the bottom of his tagboard strip. Have the youngster bend his tagboard strip ends to meet, and staple them in place. To suspend each mobile, punch holes at opposite sides atop the tagboard strip. Thread and knot a length of yarn at each hole; then tie the yarn ends together.

What A Hero!

Your youngsters may already be familiar with the modern version of Garrett Morgan's most famous invention, the electric traffic light. But do they know that this important Black American also invented a curling iron, a gas mask, and a hair-straightening cream? Many people consider Garrett Morgan a hero because his gas-mask invention saved the lives of more than 20 workers trapped in a smoke-filled tunnel in 1916. Ask your students to tell you what makes a hero. Then have each child name a person he considers a hero. Next distribute a copy of the frame pattern below to each student. Instruct each youngster to illustrate a picture of a hero and write his chosen hero's name in the space provided; then have him illustrate the border of his frame as desired. Finally have him write a few sentences about his hero on writing paper and attach them to the bottom of his frame. If desired, mount the frames on a bulletin board titled "Our Gallery Of Heroes."

Name

1856–1915
Booker T. Washington
©1998 The Education Center, Inc.

1901–1971
Louis Armstrong
©1998 The Education Center, Inc.

1820–1913
Harriet Tubman
©1998 The Education Center, Inc.

1963–
Michael Jordan
©1998 The Education Center, Inc.

1843–1929
Elijah McCoy
©1998 The Education Center, Inc.

1864–1943
George Washington Carver
©1998 The Education Center, Inc.

1913–
Rosa Parks
©1998 The Education Center, Inc.

1924–
Shirley Chisholm
©1998 The Education Center, Inc.

Fact Cards

Use with "Marvelous Mobiles" on page 17.

I am a civil rights leader.

I was arrested for refusing to give up my seat on a public bus.

I was the first Black American woman to serve in the United States Congress in Washington, D.C.

I was an inventor.

One of my inventions was a design for a lawn sprinkler.

I was a scientist.

I made more than 300 products from peanuts.

I was a famous leader of the Underground Railroad.

I helped about 300 slaves escape from slavery.

I am 6 feet 6 inches tall.

I play basketball for the Chicago Bulls.

I was a teacher.

I founded a school for Black Americans called the Tuskegee Institute.

I was a famous jazz musician.

I played the cornet and the trumpet.

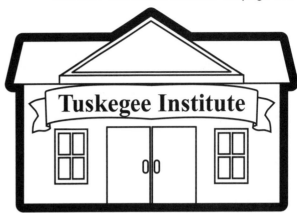

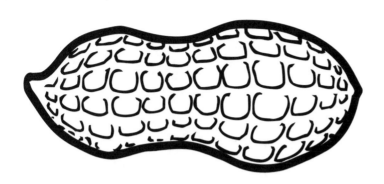

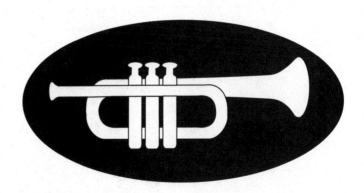

Martin Luther King, Jr.

Martin Luther King, Jr., was born on January 15, 1929, in Atlanta, Georgia. He was the second-oldest child born in his family. Martin worked very hard in high school. When he was 15 years old, he entered Morehouse College in Atlanta. A gifted speaker, Martin soon decided to become a minister. Then he went to school in Pennsylvania and in Boston. Soon Martin met Coretta Scott of Marion, Alabama. They fell in love and got married in 1953.

In 1955 Martin began to fight for *civil rights,* or the right to receive fair and equal treatment. He helped lead a protest against the Montgomery, Alabama, bus system. In 1963 Martin and other civil rights leaders planned a march in Washington, D.C. More than 200,000 people walked to the Lincoln Memorial to hear Martin's "I Have A Dream" speech. About a year later, all of Martin's hard work paid off. Congress passed the Civil Rights Act of 1964, which banned racism in public places. Later that same year, Martin was honored with the Nobel Peace Prize.

Answer the questions below.
Write each answer in a complete sentence.

1. Where was Martin Luther King, Jr., born? _____

_____

2. Where did he go to school? _____

_____

3. Whom did he marry in 1953? _____

_____

4. What did Martin Luther King, Jr., lead a protest against in 1955? _____

_____

5. What did he help plan in 1963? _____

_____

6. What was the name of the speech he gave at the Lincoln Memorial? _____

_____

7. What honor did Martin Luther King, Jr., receive in 1964? _____

_____

8. How are you like Martin Luther King, Jr.? Explain your answer. _____

_____

_____

CHINESE NEW YEAR

"Gung Hay Fat Choy!" That means "Happy New Year" in Chinese! The Chinese New Year begins with the first new moon of the year, usually between January 21 and February 19. On this date, everyone in China turns a year older, no matter what the date of his birth. Children receive small red envelopes that contain good-luck money. People light fireworks and perform a lion dance to scare away evil spirits. Children carry riddle lanterns in a traditional lantern parade. When the parade is over, the lanterns are hung in public for all to enjoy!

Dance Of The Dragon

Once a year, the dragon appears in the Chinese New Year parade. It is believed that the dragon is a symbol of goodness and strength. Have students make their own dragon masks for a New Year's parade. To make a mask, direct each student to paint a paper plate red. Assist each youngster in cutting two eyeholes in her mask as shown. Next have her cut desired decorations from red, yellow, and orange construction paper, and glue them to her plate. Then have her attach a craft stick to the back of the mask with tape. Invite your students to wear their masks and parade on in to a new year!

Marvelous Money Trees

These marvelous money trees are bound to bring good luck! Tell students that the Chinese believe money trees bring material prosperity. Money trees are created by decorating cypress or pine branches with flowers, money, and garlands of seeds and nuts. Invite your youngsters to make their own miniature versions of money trees to celebrate the new year. To make a money tree, have each student paint an eight-ounce Styrofoam® cup green. Then have him press a one-inch ball of clay into the bottom of his cup. Next direct him to press two seven-inch twigs into the clay and then fill the cup with Spanish moss. To complete his tree, have each student tape paper coins to the twigs. Your youngsters will proudly share these money trees with family members.

Easy As 1-2-3!

Teaching your students the numbers in Chinese is as easy as 1-2-3! Display a chart like the one shown. Tell students that the Chinese write numbers using diagrams called *characters*. Next show students how to write each number in Chinese. Then have each youngster paint the numbers on a large piece of white construction paper. For an added challenge, have each student write and solve simple math problems written in Chinese. "Gung Hay Fat Choy!"

一	二	三	四	五
YE (1)	ER (2)	SAN (3)	SI (4)	WU (5)
六	七	八	九	十
LIU(6)	QI (7)	BA (8)	JIU (9)	SHI (10)

Lighting The New Year

How many lanterns did Ching Lee light during the Chinese New Year celebration?
Follow the dragon trail to find out.
Write your answers in the lanterns.

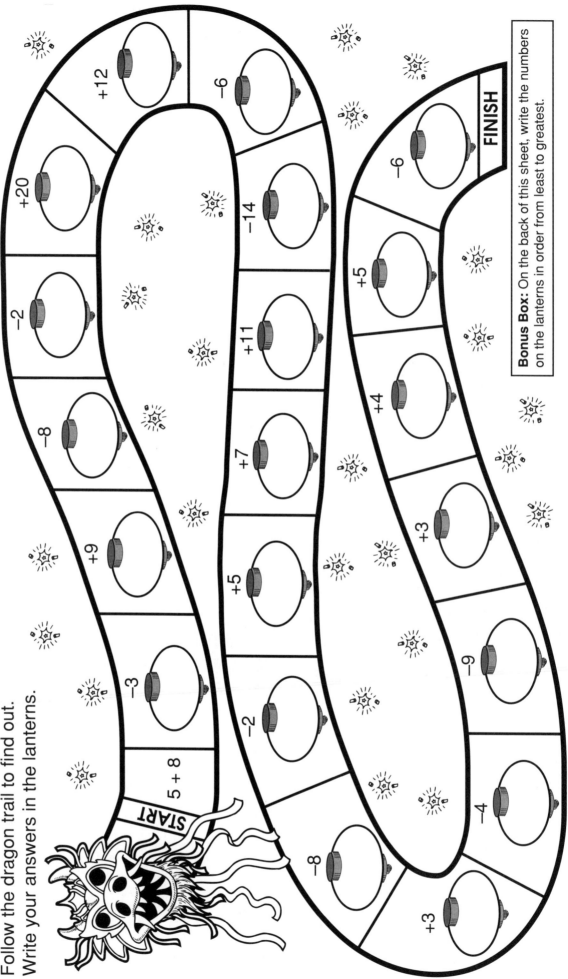

START

5 + 8

−3

+9

−8

−2

+20

+12

−6

−14

+11

+7

+5

−2

−8

+3

−4

−9

+3

+4

+5

−6

FINISH

Bonus Box: On the back of this sheet, write the numbers on the lanterns in order from least to greatest.

©1998 The Education Center, Inc. • *February Monthly Reproducibles* • Grades 2–3 • TEC941 • Key p. 63

Greetings From China!

Read the letter below.
Follow the example as you correct Sung Lee's letter.

Example: today is monday, february 9, 1998
                      T   M   F

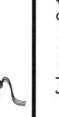

february 6 1998

dear emily

this week we celebrated our chinese new year   there was a new moon

and now i am a year older!

we had a parade on tuesday   We carried lanterns down the streets and

lit fireworks. We even saw the lion dance. it was fun

Last night we ate wontons and pudding cake. mom and dad gave me a

red envelope filled with good-luck money. Can you come visit me for our

celebration next year

your friend

sung lee

Bonus Box: On the back of this page, write a letter to Sung Lee. Remember to use correct punctuation and capital letters.

Name _____

A Bang-Up Job!

Read each firecracker.
Color the firecracker red if it tells about Chinese New Year.

sadness

gifts of money

the lion dance

firecrackers

family traditions

a television

a rainbow

a dancing dragon

happiness

new clothes

playing football

colorful kites

the color red

a new moon

a new beginning

Bonus Box: Write the underlined words in ABC order on the back of this sheet.

©1998 The Education Center, Inc. • *February Monthly Reproducibles* • Grades 2–3 • TEC941 • Key p. 63

Presidents' Day

Abraham Lincoln's birthday (February 12) and George Washington's birthday (February 22) used to be celebrated as separate holidays. Today, the country honors Lincoln, Washington, and others who have served as presidents of the United States on the third Monday in February. This federal holiday is called Presidents' Day.

A Presidential Sort

After teaching your youngsters about the presidents, have them sort these nifty fact cards! Duplicate one copy of page 28 and one construction-paper copy of pages 29 and 30 for each student. Instruct each youngster to color and cut out his pictures of Lincoln and Washington. Have him cut apart and read each sentence on his presidential fact cards; then direct him to glue each card in a space on its corresponding hat. Extend the lesson by having each youngster incorporate the facts into a story about President Lincoln or President Washington. Display the completed projects around the room for all to enjoy!

I Cannot Tell A Lie

Use the famous legend of George Washington and the cherry tree as a springboard for a writing activity. After telling the story, have your students tell you why it is important to always tell the truth. List their responses on the chalkboard. Next have each youngster complete the sentence "It is important to tell the truth because…" on a five-inch, lined cherry cutout. Invite each student to share his sentence with his classmates. Collect the pages and bind them between two red cherry covers; then add the title "We Cannot Tell A Lie" to the front cover. Place the resulting booklet at your reading center for students to read again and again.

Delightful Debates

Have your youngsters investigate debates with this delightful idea! Before his presidency, Lincoln was involved in an important slavery debate with Stephen Douglas in his run for a spot in the U.S. Senate. Tell your students that a *debate* is a discussion between two groups of people about a specific topic or idea. Enlist your students' help in creating a list of behaviors to follow when debating, such as taking turns talking, using polite manners, and respecting the opinions of others. Then select a topic from the box shown. Divide your students into two groups: one side *for* the selected topic and one side *against* it. Have the two sides debate for a specified time limit. When time has expired, have students discuss how the debate helped them understand each other's opinions. Then select another topic from the box and have students debate again!

Dogs Make The Best Pets

Gum Chewing Should Be Allowed In School

Television Is Bad For You

Going To The Movies Is Better Than Renting Videos

Playing Sports Is Better Than Playing Video Games

Presidential Fact Cards

Use with "A Presidential Sort" on page 27.

I was born in Kentucky on February 12, 1809.	In 1863 I issued the Emancipation Proclamation to free the slaves.	I was known as "Honest Abe."
Legend has it that I told the truth after cutting down a cherry tree.		
I was in charge of the American Army.		
I was the first president of the United States.		
I gave the Gettysburg Address on November 19, 1863.	I led the United States during the Civil War.	I was the 16th president of the United States.
I was elected president of the Constitutional Convention.		
I was known as the "Father Of Our Country."		
I was born in Virginia on February 22, 1732.		

Abraham Lincoln Pattern

Use with "A Presidential Sort" on page 27.

George Washington Pattern
Use with "A Presidential Sort" on page 27.

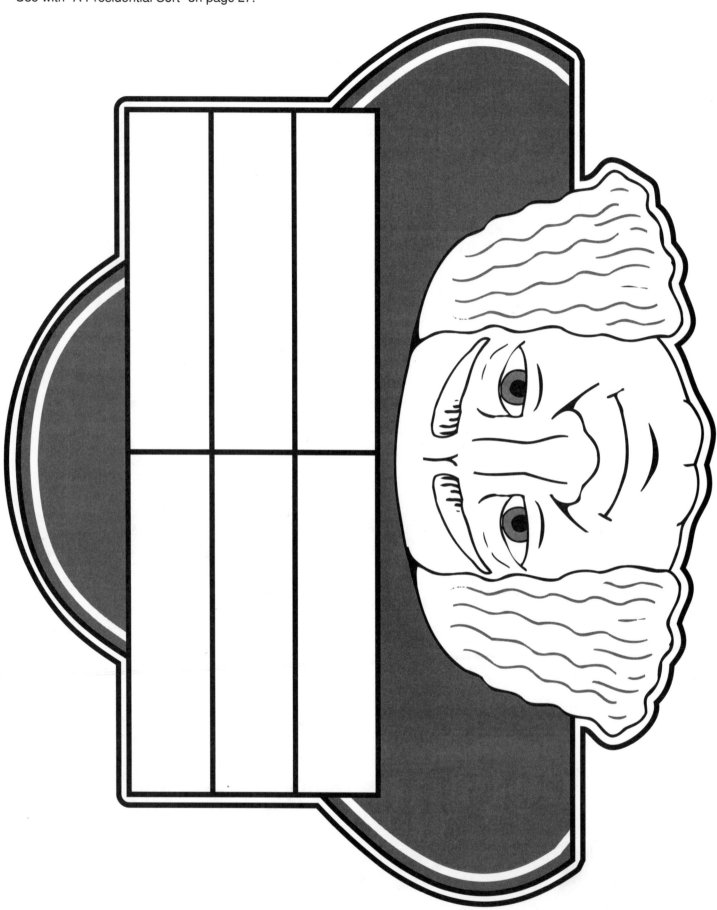

Name _____

Hats Off To Abraham Lincoln!

Count each set of coins.
Write the amount on the line.

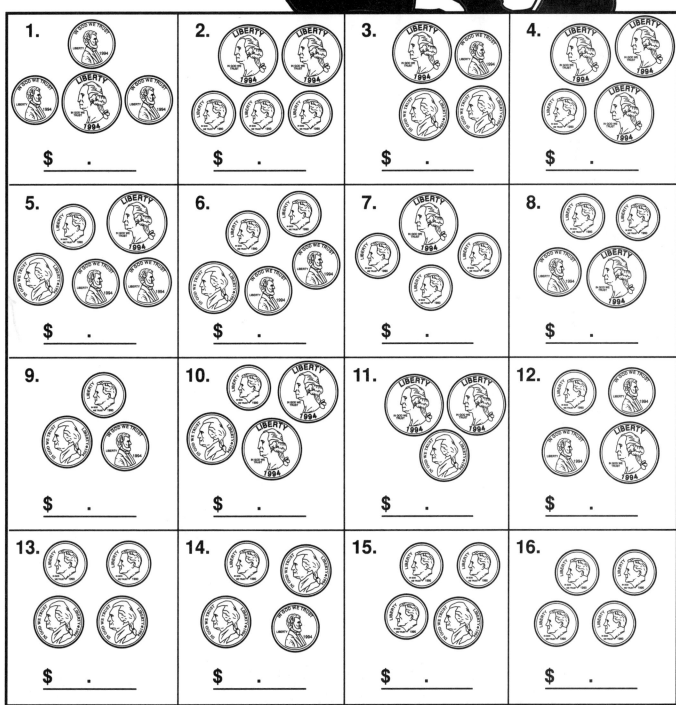

1. $ _____ . _____

2. $ _____ . _____

3. $ _____ . _____

4. $ _____ . _____

5. $ _____ . _____

6. $ _____ . _____

7. $ _____ . _____

8. $ _____ . _____

9. $ _____ . _____

10. $ _____ . _____

11. $ _____ . _____

12. $ _____ . _____

13. $ _____ . _____

14. $ _____ . _____

15. $ _____ . _____

16. $ _____ . _____

Multiplication, By George!

Solve each problem.
Color the **cherries red** as you use the answers.

3 x 5	2 x 4	4 x 3	5 x 8	2 x 7
4 x 9	5 x 3	4 x 8	3 x 8	4 x 5
2 x 8	5 x 9	5 x 5	6 x 3	4 x 4
3 x 3	4 x 6	9 x 1	3 x 7	3 x 4	2 x 6
5 x 6	3 x 9	5 x 7	4 x 2	4 x 0	2 x 5
5 x 2	2 x 3	4 x 1	5 x 1	5 x 0

5 x 4 = _____   2 x 2 = _____   2 x 9 = _____

3 x 2 = _____   8 x 1 = _____   4 x 7 = _____

FAIRY TALES

Jakob Grimm and his younger brother, Wilhelm, published 210 fairy tales between 1812 and 1857. Honor the birth of Wilhelm Grimm, born February 24, 1786, with this fanfare of fairy-tale activities and reproducibles.

Fun With Fairy Tales

These booklets will put your youngsters in-the-know with fairy tales! Duplicate one copy of the booklet pages on pages 35 and 36 for each student. Ask each youngster to personalize and illustrate the booklet cover. Then, as a class, read the fairy-tale fact on each booklet page. Have each student illustrate each fact as desired. Next distribute one white construction-paper copy of the castle pattern on page 34 to each student. Instruct him to color and cut out his pattern; then direct him to cut out his booklet cover and booklet pages. Finally have him stack the booklet cover and the booklet pages in sequential order; then staple the cover and the pages to the front of the castle pattern where indicated.

Fairy-Tale Facts

by Alex

Now That's A Tale!

Now that your youngsters know what a fairy tale is, have them write their own fairy-tale adventures! Duplicate one copy of page 37 for each student. Direct her to write a fairy tale on the lines. Challenge her to incorporate as many fairy-tale elements as she can. To complete the activity, have her glue her story atop a slightly larger sheet of colored construction paper. Collect the stories; then staple them to a bulletin board with the title "Now That's A Tale!"

Fractured Fairy Tales

What's a fractured fairy tale? Why, it's a twist on a familiar childhood story! Share a few of these delightful and humorous fairy tales with your students.

- *Cinder Edna* by Ellen Jackson (Lothrop, Lee & Shepard Books; 1994)
- *The Frog Prince Continued* by Jon Scieszka (Viking Children's Books, 1991)
- *Hanzel And Pretzel* by Mike Thaler (Scholastic Inc., 1997)
- *Prince Cinders* by Babette Cole (The Putnam & Grosset Group, 1997)
- *The Princess And The Pea-Ano* by Mike Thaler (Scholastic Inc., 1997)
- *Schmoe White And The Seven Dorfs* by Mike Thaler (Scholastic Inc., 1997)
- *Sleepless Beauty* by Frances Minters (Viking, 1996)
- *The Three Little Wolves And The Big Bad Pig* by Eugene Trivizas (Aladdin Paperbacks, 1993)
- *The True Story Of The Three Little Pigs* by Jon Scieszka (Viking Children's Books, 1989)

Castle Booklet Patterns

Staple here.

The End

©1998 The Education Center, Inc.

Staple here.

The End

©1998 The Education Center, Inc.

©1998 The Education Center, Inc. • *February Monthly Reproducibles* • Grades 2–3 • TEC941

34   **Note To The Teacher:** Use with "Fun With Fairy Tales" on page 33.

Fairy-Tale Facts

by _____

©1998 The Education Center, Inc.

Fairy tales usually begin with "Once upon a time" and "Long ago."

1.

They take place in faraway places.

2.

Fairy tales often have magic and supernatural elements,

3.

and contain the numbers 3 and 7.

4.

But fairy tales usually aren't about fairies!

5.

©1998 The Education Center, Inc. • *February Monthly Reproducibles* • Grades 2–3 • TEC941

- -

Note To The Teacher: Use with "Fun With Fairy Tales" on page 33.

Booklet Pages

And sometimes they have unusual names.

8.

But in the end, the good character lives "happily ever after"!

11.

and usually heroes and heroines.

7.

And some of them are put under spells that only love and kindness can reverse.

10.

Fairy tales often have kings and queens,

6.

Some characters are good and some are bad.

9.

Note To The Teacher: Use with "Fun With Fairy Tales" on page 33.

_____

_____

_____

_____

_____

_____

_____

_____

_____

_____

_____

_____

_____

Note To The Teacher: Use with "Now That's A Tale!" on page 33.

A Royal Salute!

Cut out the crowns below.
Put a drop of glue on each ● .
Glue each crown on its antonym.

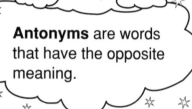

Antonyms are words that have the opposite meaning.

1.
over

2.
cry

3.
slow

4.
more

5.
rough

6.
take

7.
sink

8.
old

Bonus Box: On the back of this page, write three more antonym pairs; then write a sentence for each pair.

©1998 The Education Center, Inc. • *February Monthly Reproducibles* • Grades 2–3 • TEC941 • Key p. 63

fast   smooth   less   new   float   under   laugh   give

CANDY GALORE!

Your youngsters won't be able to resist these mouthwatering activities! Since February usually brings a lot of love *and* a lot of candy, this cache of ideas and reproducibles is sure to bring a smile to every student's face!

Candy-O!

Make the most of word skills with a fun game of Candy-O! Duplicate one copy of the lotto gameboard (page 40) for each student. Display a list of sight words in a prominent location. Have each student randomly program his gameboard with words from the list. Then read aloud each word at random. Have each youngster mark his grid with a candy marker, like M&M's®, Reese's Pieces®, Skittles® candies, or red hots. When a youngster marks five in a row, he calls out, "Candy-O!" Challenge the winning student to read or spell his words to the rest of his classmates; then reward him with a sticker or another small treat. Have students clear their boards for additional rounds of fun. When play has ended, invite your youngsters to eat their edible markers. Yum!

Hearty Tales

Turn your youngsters on to writing with conversation hearts! Program the top of a sheet of writing paper with four hearts and duplicate one copy for each student. Have each student select four conversation hearts from a bag. Have her read the message on each heart and copy it onto her paper; then have her color the hearts as desired. Next instruct her to write a story that incorporates the messages on the hearts. Encourage students to share their stories with their classmates. Collect the stories; then mount them on a bulletin board titled "Hearty Tales."

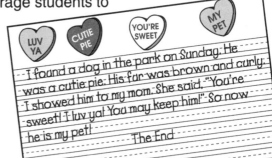

Candy-Bar Creations

Get students' creative juices flowing with these candy-bar creations. Share a variety of candy-bar wrappers with your students. Encourage youngsters to discuss the contents of the candy bars and what the wrappers look like. Then challenge each youngster to design his own candy bar. Have each student think of a name for his candy bar; then have him design and color a wrapper for his bar on a 4" x 6" strip of white construction paper. Next direct the youngster to write a description of his candy bar on an index card and attach it to his strip. If desired, invite your students to snack on miniature candy bars as they design their scrumptious creations!

Candy-O!

Make a Candy-O card.
Write one word in each box.

		Free Space		

Note To The Teacher: Use with "Candy-O!" on page 39.

Sweet Surprises

Write the correct abbreviation below each word.
Use the abbreviations in the Word Bank.

4.
Doctor
_____

3.
August
_____

2.
Avenue
_____

1.
November
_____

8.
Mister
_____

7.
September
_____

6.
Wednesday
_____

5.
Friday
_____

12.
Street
_____

11.
Tuesday
_____

10.
Road
_____

9.
October
_____

16.
Sunday
_____

15.
March
_____

14.
February
_____

13.
Missus
_____

Word Bank

Mar.	Sat.	Sun.
St.	Ave.	Thurs.
Aug.	Mon.	Dr.
Wed.	Sept.	Oct.
Tues.	Mrs.	Mr.
Nov.	Apr.	Feb.
Rd.	Fri.	

18.
April
_____

17.
Monday
_____

20.
Saturday
_____

19.
Thursday
_____

Name_____

Candy, Candy, Candy!

Graph the number of children who love candies.

Use the information in the box.

mints	10
kisses	11
lollipops	6
gum	5
candy hearts	9
candy bars	12

Kids Love Candies!

Number Of Kids

12
11
10
9
8
7
6
5
4
3
2
1
0

lollipops   kisses   mints   candy hearts   gum   candy bars

Kinds Of Candies

Use the graph to answer these questions.

1. Which candy is liked by the most children? _____

2. Which candy is liked by the least children? _____

3. How many children like gum?_____

4. How many more children like mints than lollipops? _____

5. How many more children like kisses than candy hearts ? _____

6. Which three candies are liked by the most children? _____

Bonus Box: How many children altogether like kisses, gum, and mints? _____

National Children's Dental Health Month

Are you searching for some fun dental health activities for students to sink their teeth into? Then look no further! Celebrate National Children's Dental Health Month with this unique collection of learning activities.

A Toothy Graph

Losing teeth tends to generate a lot of excitement in young students. Capitalize on these feelings by having your youngsters make this one-of-a-kind graph. Draw a bar-graph outline on a colored piece of poster board. Label each column of the graph as shown; then add a title and other needed programming. Direct each youngster to glue a personalized, tooth-shaped cutout in the appropriate column on the graph. Then evaluate the resulting graph with the class. Culminate the activity by having each youngster pen a story about a time he lost a tooth. Mount the stories around the graph for a "tooth-eriffic" display!

Tic-Tac-Tooth

Your students will enjoy this toothy version of tic-tac-toe. Duplicate one copy of page 44 for every two students. Then have students play Tic-Tac-Tooth in pairs. Before play, have each pair cut its game sheet in half on the bold line. Then instruct students to set one gameboard aside. To begin play, have each youngster choose either *X* or *O*. The *X* player begins the first game by choosing a problem to solve. The student then writes the answer under the problem, circles the tooth with that answer, and puts an *X* in the box. Next the *O* player chooses a problem to answer in the same manner. Play continues until one person scores tic-tac-tooth or until every problem has been answered. For additional practice, challenge your students to another game of Tic-Tac-Tooth using the second gameboard.

What A Smile!

These healthful snacks will persuade students to eat foods without added sugars. Tell your youngsters that sugary foods contribute to tooth decay. Then explain that dentists recommend that people snack on fresh fruits and vegetables, cheeses, and nuts. Next have each youngster snack on a healthful face. To make a face, have each student place the following items on a paper circle, or a paper plate, to resemble a face: sliced cucumber eyes with raisin pupils, a baby carrot nose, an orange smile, and mini-pretzel hair. Encourage your students to name additional nonsugary snacks as they munch on their healthful smiles. Yum!

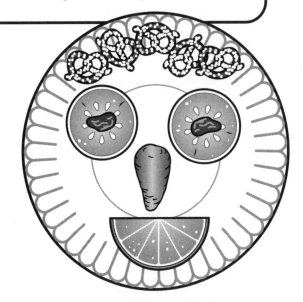

2-digit addition and subtraction with regrouping

Tic-Tac-Tooth

Teeth: 45 76 65 91 | 24 25 64 69 35

Teeth: 96 66 30 37 | 19 61 38 15 81

$$\begin{array}{r} 94 \\ -18 \\ \hline \end{array} \qquad \begin{array}{r} 35 \\ +29 \\ \hline \end{array} \qquad \begin{array}{r} 84 \\ -39 \\ \hline \end{array} \qquad \begin{array}{r} 44 \\ +17 \\ \hline \end{array} \qquad \begin{array}{r} 41 \\ -26 \\ \hline \end{array} \qquad \begin{array}{r} 38 \\ +28 \\ \hline \end{array}$$

$$\begin{array}{r} 39 \\ +26 \\ \hline \end{array} \qquad \begin{array}{r} 50 \\ -25 \\ \hline \end{array} \qquad \begin{array}{r} 40 \\ -16 \\ \hline \end{array} \qquad \begin{array}{r} 74 \\ -36 \\ \hline \end{array} \qquad \begin{array}{r} 17 \\ +13 \\ \hline \end{array} \qquad \begin{array}{r} 85 \\ -48 \\ \hline \end{array}$$

$$\begin{array}{r} 53 \\ -18 \\ \hline \end{array} \qquad \begin{array}{r} 66 \\ +25 \\ \hline \end{array} \qquad \begin{array}{r} 85 \\ -16 \\ \hline \end{array} \qquad \begin{array}{r} 33 \\ +48 \\ \hline \end{array} \qquad \begin{array}{r} 44 \\ -25 \\ \hline \end{array} \qquad \begin{array}{r} 79 \\ +17 \\ \hline \end{array}$$

©1998 The Education Center, Inc. • February Monthly Reproducibles • Grades 2–3 • TEC941 • Key p. 64

Note To The Teacher: Use with "Tic-Tac-Tooth" on page 43.

Toothy Comparisons

Read the numbers on the teeth.
Write > or < on the middle tooth.

1.  56 · 560

2.  329 · 923

3.  18 · 81

4.  47 · 67

5.  99 · 999

6.  258 · 158

7.  39 · 49

8.  701 · 107

9.  663 · 336

10.  103 · 301

11.  25 · 52

12. 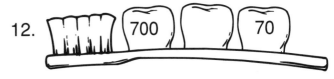 700 · 70

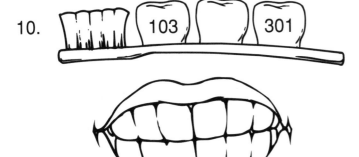

Dazzling Dental Coordinates

Write the coordinate for each picture on the map.

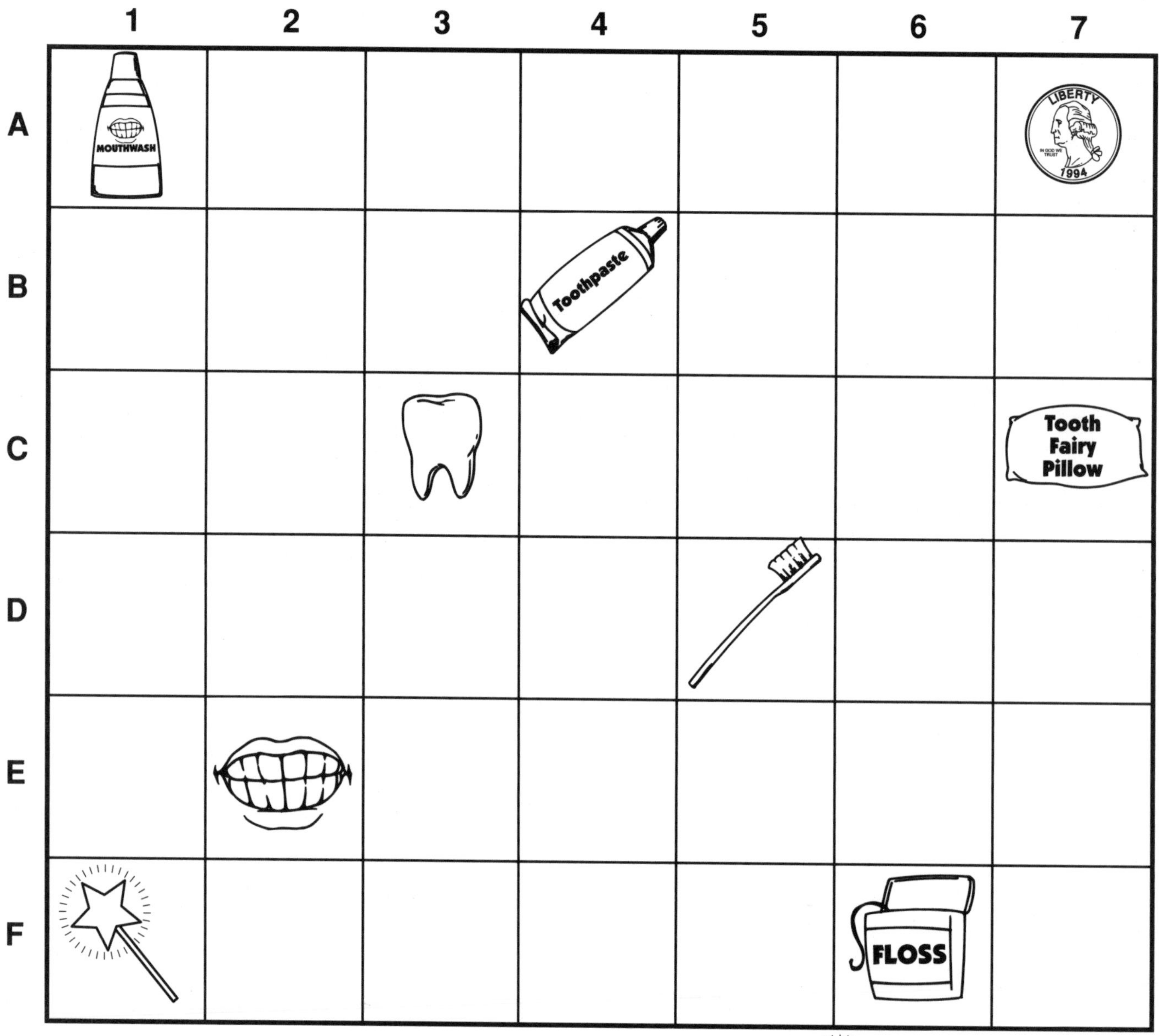

	1	2	3	4	5	6	7
A	MOUTHWASH						LIBERTY 1994
B				Toothpaste			
C			(tooth)				Tooth Fairy Pillow
D					(toothbrush)		
E		(teeth)					
F	(star wand)					FLOSS	

(teeth) _____

FLOSS _____

(star wand) _____

(tooth) _____

FLOSS _____

(toothbrush) _____

LIBERTY 1994 _____

MOUTHWASH _____

Tooth Fairy Pillow _____

Toothpaste _____

Bonus Box: Choose three items from the map. On the back of this paper, write how each item relates to dental health.

NATIONAL SNACK FOOD MONTH

Encourage students to eat healthful, nutritious snacks with this collection of fresh ideas. Before long, your students will realize there is more to snacks than just cookies, pretzels, soda, and candy!

Healthful Collages

These collages are a great way for students to learn how to choose healthful snacks. Ask your students to name the snacks they eat after school. Write their responses on the chalkboard. As a class, sort the foods into healthful and unhealthful choices. Have students name additional healthful snacks and add them to the list. Then have students create a healthful snack collage. To make his collage, have each student cut pictures of healthful snacks from magazines and glue them to a paper plate. Serve apple wedges or crackers and cheese as students create their collages.

What A Choice!

You can count on this cooperative-group activity to persuade students to eat healthful snacks. Challenge each youngster to write down every snack she eats over the course of one week. At the end of the week, have students evaluate their lists. Divide students into small groups. Have each youngster share her list with her group. Encourage students to discuss the healthful and unhealthful snack choices. Now that's a great way to reinforce good nutrition!

Radical Raisins!

What better way to reinforce the concept of making healthful snack choices than with raisins! Tell your students that raisins are a good source of vitamins and minerals. Raisins also provide the body with a good source of quick energy. Next copy the following activities onto poster board. Place the poster, writing paper, and a supply of snack-size raisin boxes at a center. Have each student complete the tasks with a box of raisins. Learning about healthful snack choices has never been more fun!

1. Estimate the number of raisins in your box. Write the estimate on your paper.
2. Round your estimate to the nearest ten. Write the answer on your paper.
3. Now open your box of raisins. Count your raisins. Were you close to your estimate?
4. Count your raisins by twos, threes, fives, and tens.
5. Draw a picture of a raisin on your paper. List three reasons why raisins are good snack choices.
6. Write a recipe that includes raisins.
7. Now eat your raisins!

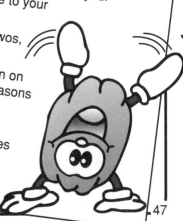

A Healthful Basket

Look at the number on each healthful food.
Round the number to the nearest ten.
Write your answer on the line.
Color by the code.

One answer has been
done for you!

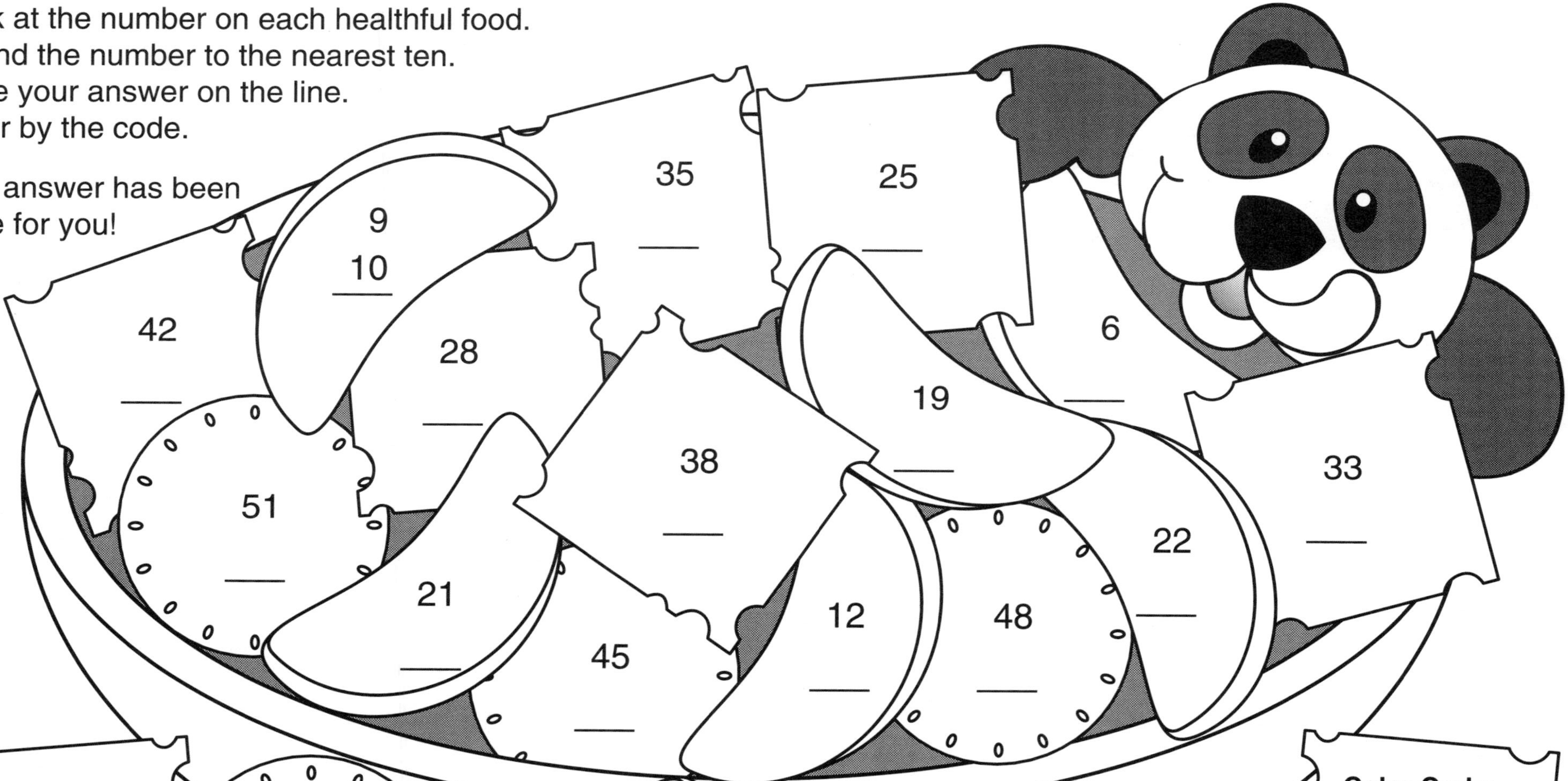

33 ___

6 ___

22 ___

25 ___

19 ___

48 ___

35 ___

38 ___

12 ___

45 ___

9
10 ___

28 ___

21 ___

42 ___

51 ___

Remember:
Look at the
ones place in
each number.

Round up if the
number is **five
or more.**

Round down if
the number is
four or less

©1998 The Education Center, Inc. • February Monthly Reproducibles • Grades 2–3 • TEC941 • Key p. 64

Color Code:
10 = red
20 = green
30 = yellow
40 = orange
50 = light brown

Petey's Popcorn

Help Petey put his popcorn together.
Look at each word.
Cut and paste the homophone.

Homophone: One of two or more words that sound alike but have different spellings and meanings.

1. ate

2. see

3. pain

4. blue

5. sale

6. right

7. so

8. pair

9. here

10. deer

©1998 The Education Center, Inc. • *February Monthly Reproducibles* • Grades 2–3 • TEC941 • Key p. 64

hear

blew

eight

pear

dear

sea

sail

sew

write

pane

Great Grapes!

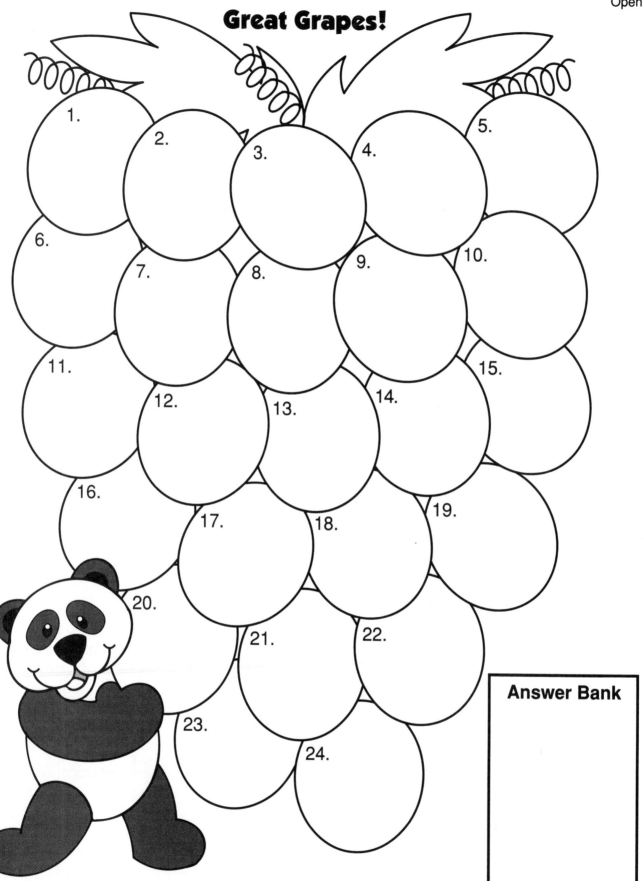

Answer Bank

Note To The Teacher: Duplicate one copy of this page and program it as desired. Then duplicate copies for your students.

Responsible Pet Owner Month

Promote dependable pet ownership by celebrating Responsible Pet Owner Month. This unique collection of activities will help students understand the important role we play in our pets' lives.

Caring For Pets

These adorable booklets are an excellent way for students to learn about caring for pets. Duplicate one copy of pages 52, 53, and 54 for each student. Direct each youngster to personalize and color the dog-bowl pattern, title page, and "illustrated by" page. Then have each student cut out the dog-bowl pattern. Next read aloud each pet-care pointer. Ask students to discuss the importance of each pointer; then have them illustrate each one as desired. Next instruct students to cut apart the booklet pages and assemble them, in order, behind the booklet cover. Then help each youngster staple his booklet to the dog-bowl pattern as shown. Now those are pet-care pointers students can really count on!

My Pet And Me

Pay a tribute to pets with this unique project. Have each student trace a large circle template on a nine-inch square of drawing paper. Then have him draw a portrait of himself and his pet (or a pet he would like to have) inside the circle. Instruct him to cut out the circle and mount it on a nine-inch square of colored construction paper. Then have the student write his name and the name of his pet at the top of his portrait. Next have each youngster write about his pet on writing paper; then have him attach his sentences to the bottom of his portrait. Invite each youngster to share his portrait and sentences with his classmates. Then mount the completed portraits on a bulletin board titled "My Pet And Me."

Classifying Pets

Use your students' interests in pets to provide classification practice. Ask each student to bring a picture of her pet to school. (For a student who may not own a pet, have her bring in a magazine picture of a pet she would like to own.) Mount the pictures on the chalkboard. Next ask students for some grouping ideas, such as color, size, tail or no tail, fur or no fur, or scales or no scales. Then enlist students' help in putting the pet pictures into different groups. For an added challenge, have your youngsters suggest groups for classifying pets into three categories, such as long tail, short tail, or no tail. For additional classification practice, place the pictures at a center for students to sort on their own.

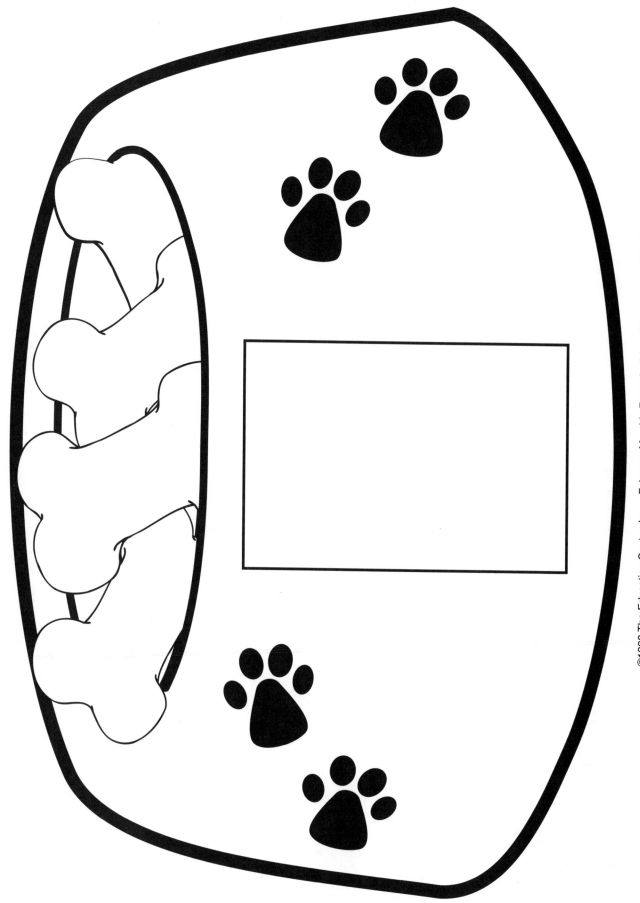

52

Note To The Teacher: Use with "Caring For Pets" on page 51.

All pets need food and water,

A pet needs a clean environment.

🦴 2

🦴 6

Owning a pet is a big responsibility.

Some pets need grooming.

🦴 1

🦴 5

Illustrated by

_____

Most pets need exercise.

🦴 4

Caring For Pets

and lots of love.

🦴 3

©1998 The Education Center, Inc. • *February Monthly Reproducibles* • Grades 2–3 • TEC941

Note To The Teacher: Use with "Caring For Pets" on page 51.

53

Training a pet takes patience

10

and your pet will love you!

14

Some pets can be trained.

9

you will love your pet,

13

Regular visits to the veterinarian are very important.

8

If you are a good pet owner,

12

Sometimes there is additional cleanup, too.

7

and lots of love.

11

Note To The Teacher: Use with "Caring For Pets" on page 51.

NATIONAL PANCAKE WEEK

National Pancake Week is observed the week of *Shrove* or *Pancake Tuesday* (the day before Ash Wednesday). During this week, people traditionally cook and eat flat, thin pancakes. On February 9, 1975, the largest pancake was flipped on a giant griddle in Liberal, Kansas. It was 12 feet in diameter!

A Pat On The Pancake!

Cook up a little pancake fun with this unique learning center! Cut out a supply of tan construction-paper pancakes and yellow construction-paper pats of butter. Laminate each cutout. Then use a permanent marker to program each pancake with an addition problem. Program each pat of butter with a different numeral to correspond to the sum of each addition fact. To use this center, a child chooses a pancake and works out the problem on scrap paper. When he knows the answer, he places the corresponding pat of butter atop the pancake. For older students, program pancakes with two-digit addition or subtraction problems. Now that's a center students will give a pat on the pancake!

Pass The Pancake

This fun version of Hot Potato will have your youngsters flipping over flapjacks! Cut a pancake from tan construction paper and glue it to a Styrofoam® tray. To play the game, have students stand in a large circle. Ask youngsters to pass the pancake while music is played aloud. When the music stops, have the child holding the pancake sit down. Continue play until only one student is remaining. Then invite all students to stand up and play the game again!

Fantastic Flapjacks!

Tempt your students' taste buds with these easy-to-make pancakes! Gather a large mixing bowl, an electric griddle, a spatula, and the ingredients for the Chocolate Chip Pancakes. Invite your students to assist you in preparing the batter for the pancakes. Then sit back and enjoy these fantastic flapjacks!

Chocolate Chip Pancakes

(makes 10–12 small pancakes)

1 cup biscuit mix
3/4 cup milk
1 egg, beaten
1/2 tsp. oil
1/2 cup chocolate chips
toppings (butter, syrup, and powdered sugar)

Spray a nonstick spray on the griddle. Preheat the griddle to 375°F. Mix the first five ingredients together. Pour the mixture by tablespoonfuls onto the heated griddle. Flip the pancake when the top is bubbling. Serve the pancakes warm, topped with butter, syrup, and powdered sugar.

Pancake Punctuation

Color the pancake that shows the missing punctuation.

1. Sam likes to make breakfast

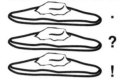
.
?
!

2. Can you guess what Sam makes

.
?
!

3. Sam makes pancakes

.
?
!

4. Boy, he makes a lot of pancakes

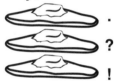
.
?
!

5. Sam loves pancakes

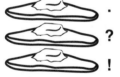
.
?
!

6. Do you know why Sam loves pancakes

.
?
!

7. He loves them because they taste good

.
?
!

8. Do you like to eat pancakes

.
?
!

9. Sam likes pancakes with butter

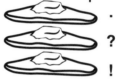
.
?
!

10. He likes them with syrup, too

.
?
!

11. Sometimes he eats too much

.
?
!

12. Boy, that makes Sam's tummy hurt

.
?
!

Bonus Box: On the back of this paper, draw and color a picture of Sam making pancakes. Write two sentences that tell about your picture.

Punny Pancakes

Read the riddle below.
Add or subtract. Show your work.

Riddle: What is a pancake's favorite fairy tale?

1. 48 + 23 (L)	2. 50 − 25 (A)	3. 71 − 35 (A)	4. 19 + 11 (S)
5. 97 − 18 (D)	6. 27 + 18 (G)	7. 80 − 52 (L)	8. 91 − 73 (R)
9. 57 − 28 (H)	10. 31 + 29 (E)	11. 63 − 24 (E)	12. 38 + 16 (N)
13. 39 + 55 (I)	14. 19 + 31 (N)	15. 59 + 11 (D)	16. 62 − 46 (D)

Write the letter that matches each answer to discover the answer to the riddle.

Answer:

"____ ____ ____ ____ ____ ____ ____ ____ ____ ____ ____ ____ ____ ____ ____ ____"
29 36 54 30 39 71 25 50 16   45 18 94 79 70 28 60

Pancakes Aplenty

Use the code to color the pancakes.
Answer the questions below.
Use the graph.

Color Code:
Color the pancake **brown.**
Color the butter **yellow.**
Color the syrup **red.**

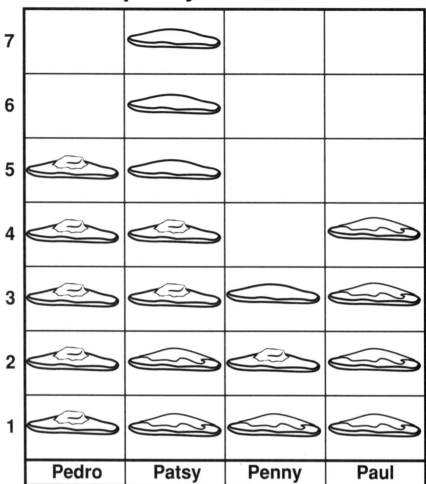

1. Who ate the most pancakes? _____

2. Who ate the fewest pancakes? _____

3. Who ate the most pancakes with butter? _____

4. Who ate the fewest pancakes with butter? _____

5. Who ate the most pancakes with syrup? _____

6. Who ate the fewest pancakes with syrup? _____

7. How many pancakes did Pedro and Penny eat altogether? _____

8. How many pancakes did Patsy and Paul eat altogether? _____

9. How many more pancakes did Pedro eat than Paul? _____

10. Who ate one more pancake than Penny? _____

11. Who ate two more pancakes than Pedro? _____

12. How many more pancakes did Patsy eat than Penny? _____

©1998 The Education Center, Inc. • *February Monthly Reproducibles* • Grades 2–3 • TEC941 • Key p. 64

International Friendship Week

Inspire students to form lasting friendships with others during International Friendship Week, held the last week in February. These friendly activities will foster caring and unity among your students.

Friendship Pennants

Help your youngsters investigate friendship with these one-of-a-kind pennants. To begin, tell students that friends often pay each other compliments, such as "I like your dress," or "You did a nice job on the test." Ask your students to name additional compliments. Then have each youngster make a friendship pennant. Instruct each student to write his name in the middle of a large pennant cutout. Then divide students into groups of five. Tell each child to pass his pennant to the student seated to his right. Next have him write a compliment about the child whose pennant is in front of him; then have him pass the pennant again. Continue to have each youngster write a compliment on a pennant until his own pennant has been returned. Then display the completed pennants around the room for all to enjoy.

He is a good listener.

Eric

He's a good soccer player.

He makes friends easily.

He is nice.

Friendly Letters

Review letter writing *and* promote lasting friendships with this kid-friendly activity. Write a friendly letter on a sheet of chart paper and display it in a prominent location. Then review the parts of a friendly letter by asking students to point out the date, greeting, body, closing, and signature on the displayed chart. Next have each youngster write a friendly letter to a buddy on writing paper. Once her letter is written, direct her to check it to make sure she included each part. Next assist students in editing their letters for clarity and punctuation. Then encourage each youngster to hand-deliver or mail her letter to her buddy.

A Friendly Swap

Have your youngsters make these unique pins to swap with a friend. Copy the poem shown onto paper, and duplicate one for each student. Also provide each youngster with one large safety pin and five craft beads. To make a friendship pin, have each youngster open his pin and slide his beads onto the pointed end. Next have him close his pin and tape it onto his copy of the poem. Then invite each child to swap his pin with a friend. Help each student attach his pin to his shirt. Then encourage youngsters to introduce their friends to their classmates. What a nice way to make lasting friendships!

A friend you are.
Special friends we'll be.
This friendship pin
Is to you from me!

60 Name _____

Frankie's Friendly Letter

Help Frankie write a friendly letter to his friend Fiona.
Look at the Word Bank.
Write the correct synonym in each blank.

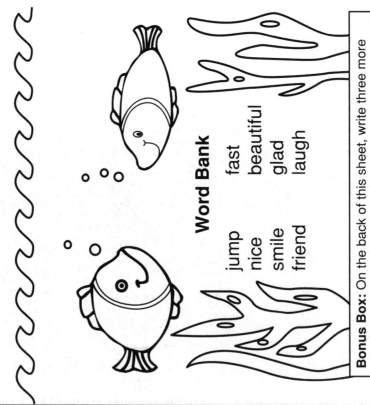

Remember:
Synonyms are words that have the same or almost the same meanings.

Word Bank

jump	fast
nice	beautiful
smile	glad
friend	laugh

Dear Fiona,

I am _____ I know you. You are _____ .
   (happy)   (kind)

You also have _____ scales. You can swim
              (pretty)

_____ and _____ high.
(quickly)   (leap)

I _____ every time I see you. You make me
  (grin)

_____ .
(giggle)

Your _____ ,
      (pal)

Frankie

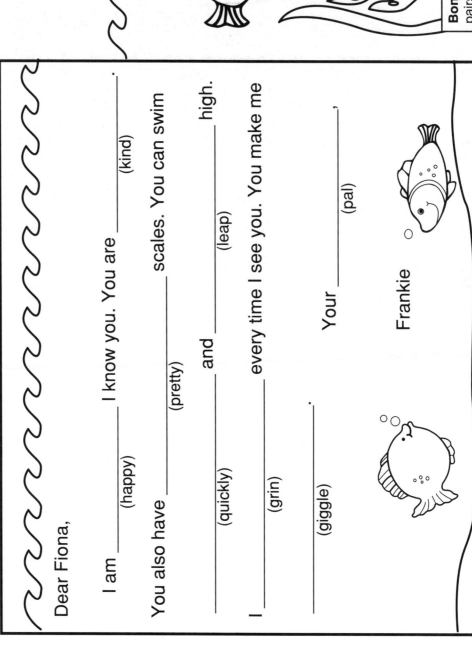

Bonus Box: On the back of this sheet, write three more pairs of synonyms. Then write a sentence using each word.

Long-Distance Friendship

Who has the longest long-distance friendship?
Use a ruler to measure these lines in centimeters.
Write the measurements in the boxes below the lines.
Then add the measurements in each row, and write the totals in the blanks.

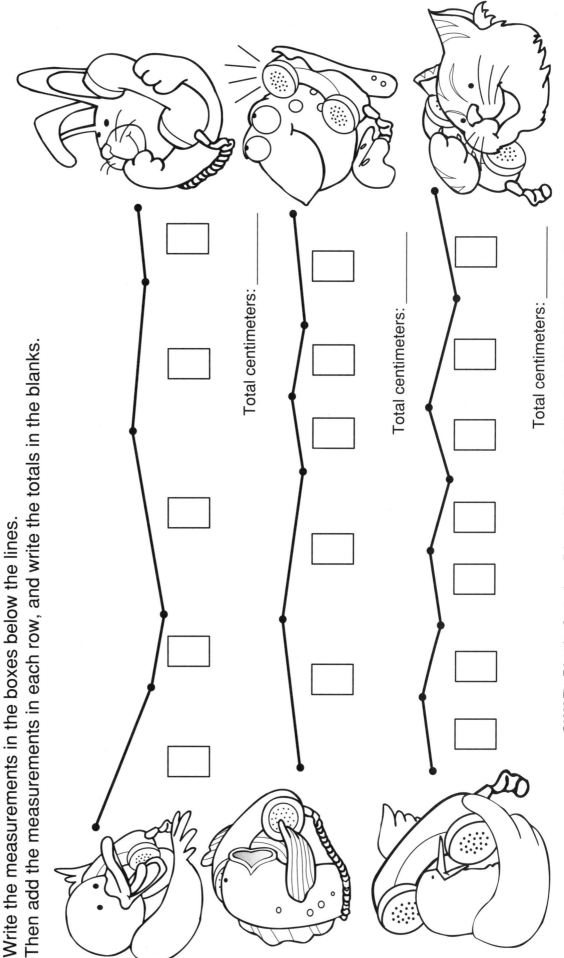

Total centimeters: _____

Total centimeters: _____

Total centimeters: _____

Name _____

Best Of Friends!

Read the paragraph.
Use the information in the paragraph to complete the diagram.
Write words or phrases on the diagram below.

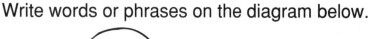

Dudley Duck and Betsy Bunny are best friends. They do everything together! They both like to play in the afternoon sun. Dudley and Betsy enjoy taking walks around the pond. On rainy days Betsy likes to sit under a tree and watch Dudley dive up and down in the water. Betsy does not like water as much as Dudley does! Sometimes Dudley and Betsy sit in the grass and watch the clouds. They like to look for cloud animals. Betsy likes to look for bunnies and Dudley likes to look for ducks.

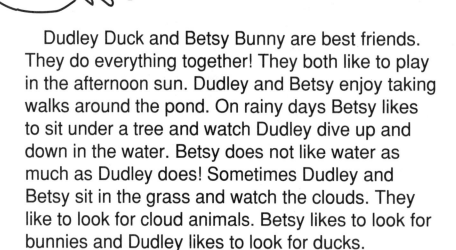

Both

Dudley

Betsy

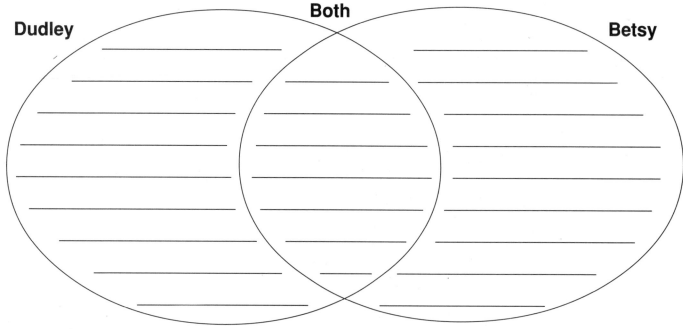

Answer Keys

Page 6

ROW A 1 0 3 3 5 2   ROW D 5 4 3 2 2 5
ROW B 3 5 2 4 5 3   ROW E 4 4   4 0
ROW C 3 5 2 1 2 3

Bonus Box:

3 x 3 = 9	4 x 3 = 12	5 x 3 = 15
3 x 4 = 12	4 x 4 = 16	5 x 4 = 20
3 x 5 = 15	4 x 5 = 20	5 x 5 = 25

Page 7

1. fact   2. opinion   3. fact   4. fact   5. opinion
6. opinion   7. fact   8. fact   9. fact   10. fact

Page 10

1. aren't   2. I'm   3. you've   4. you're   5. it'll   6. they've
7. we're   8. he'd   9. hadn't   10. I'd   11. doesn't   12. she'll
13. you'll   14. they'd   15. let's   16. wouldn't

Page 11

arrows	cookies
heart	flowers
hug	friend
love	pink
valentine	smile

candy	card
Cupid	crush
red	kisses
roses	surprise
wishes	sweets

Page 12

*Answers will vary in each of these rows.

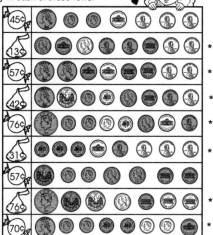

Page 15

cherries (purple)	cookies (red)	hearts (red)	candies (purple)
kisses (pink)	roses (red)	wishes (pink)	cards (red)
hugs (red)	boxes (pink)	arrows (red)	crushes (pink)

Page 22

Answers may vary.

1. He was born in Atlanta, Georgia.
2. He went to Morehouse College in Atlanta. He also went to school in Pennsylvania and Boston.
3. He married Coretta Scott.
4. He led a protest against the Montgomery bus system.
5. He helped plan a march in Washington, D.C.
6. The name of the speech was "I Have A Dream."
7. He received the Nobel Peace Prize.
8. Answers will vary.

Page 24

START 10 19 11 9 29 41 35 21 32 39 44 42 34 37 33 24 27 31 36 30 **FINISH**

Bonus Box: 9, 10, 11, 19, 21, 24, 27, 29, 30, 31, 32, 33, 34, 35, 36, 37, 39, 41, 42, 44

Page 25

D E   F
~~dear emily~~,   ~~february 6~~,1998
      T   C   N   Y   T

~~this~~ week we celebrated our ~~chinese new year~~. ~~there~~ was a new moon
        I
and now ~~i~~ am a year older!
   W   T

~~we~~ had a parade on ~~tuesday~~. We carried lanterns down the streets and

lit fireworks. We even saw the lion dance. ~~it~~ was fun!
                                          M   D

    Last night we ate wontons and pudding cake. ~~mom~~ and ~~dad~~ gave me a

red envelope filled with good-luck money. Can you come visit me for our

celebration next year ?
                                          Y

                              ~~your friend~~,
                        S   L
                        ~~sung lee~~

Page 26

<u>beginning</u> clothes <u>dragon</u> <u>firecrackers</u> football <u>gifts</u> <u>happiness</u> <u>kites</u> <u>lion</u> <u>moon</u> rainbow <u>red</u> sadness television <u>traditions</u>

Underlined words are colored red.

Page 31

1. $.28   2. $.80   3. $.36   4. $.85
5. $.42   6. $.27   7. $.55   8. $.46
9. $.16   10. $.65   11. $.55   12. $.37
13. $.30   14. $.21   15. $.35   16. $.40

Page 32

Solve each problem.
Color the **cherries red** as you use the answers.

3 x5 = 15	2 x4 = 8	4 x3 = 12	5 x8 = 40	2 x7 = 14
4 x9 = 36	5 x3 = 15	4 x8 = 32	3 x8 = 24	4 x5 = 20
2 x8 = 16	5 x9 = 45	5 x5 = 25	6 x3 = 18	4 x4 = 16
3 x3 = 9	4 x6 = 24	9 x1 = 9	3 x7 = 21	3 x4 = 12	2 x6 = 12
5 x6 = 30	3 x9 = 27	5 x7 = 35	4 x2 = 8	4 x0 = 0	2 x5 = 10
5 x2 = 10	2 x3 = 6	4 x1 = 4	5 x1 = 5	5 x0 = 0

5 x 4 = 20   2 x 2 = 4   2 x 9 = 18

3 x 2 = 6   8 x 1 = 8   4 x 7 = 28

Page 38

1. under   2. laugh   3. fast   4. less
5. smooth   6. give   7. float   8. new

Page 41

1. Nov.   2. Ave.   3. Aug.   4. Dr.   5. Fri.   6. Wed.   7. Sept.
8. Mr.   9. Oct.   10. Rd.   11. Tues.   12. St.   13. Mrs.   14. Feb.
15. Mar.   16. Sun.   17. Mon.   18. Apr.   19. Thurs.   20. Sat.

Answer Keys

Page 42

Kids Love Candies!

(Bar graph with vertical axis "Number Of Kids" from 0 to 12, horizontal axis "Kinds Of Candies" with categories: lollipops, kisses, mints, candy hearts, gum, candy bars)

1. candy bars
2. gum
3. five
4. four
5. two
6. mints, kisses, candy bars

Bonus Box: 26

Page 44

38 + 28 = 66	41 − 26 = 15	44 + 17 = 61	84 − 39 = 45	35 + 29 = 64	94 − 18 = 76
85 − 48 = 37	17 + 13 = 30	74 − 36 = 38	40 − 16 = 24	50 − 25 = 25	39 + 26 = 65
79 + 17 = 96	44 − 25 = 19	33 + 48 = 81	85 − 16 = 69	66 + 25 = 91	53 − 18 = 35

Page 45

1. <   2. <   3. <   4. <   5. <   6. >
7. <   8. >   9. >   10. <   11. <   12. >

Page 46

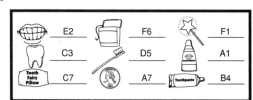

E2, F6, F1, C3, D5, A1, C7, A7, B4

Page 48

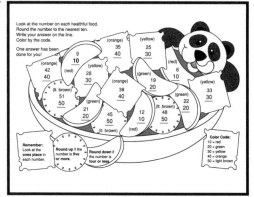

Page 49

1. eight   2. sea   3. pane   4. blew   5. sail
6. write   7. sew   8. pear   9. hear   10. dear

Page 56

1. . or !   4. !   7. . or !   10. .
2. ?   5. . or !   8. ?   11. . or !
3. .   6. ?   9. .   12. !

Page 57

1. 71   2. 25   3. 36   4. 30
5. 79   6. 45   7. 28   8. 18
9. 29   10. 60   11. 39   12. 54
13. 94   14. 50   15. 70   16. 16

HANSEL AND "GRIDDLE"

Page 58

The graph is colored according to the Color Code.

1. Patsy   2. Penny   3. Pedro   4. Paul   5. Paul   6. Pedro
7. 8   8. 11   9. 1   10. Paul   11. Patsy   12. 4

Page 60

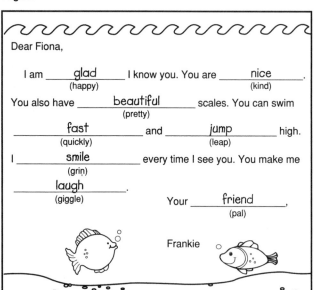

Dear Fiona,

I am ___glad___ (happy) I know you. You are ___nice___ (kind).

You also have ___beautiful___ (pretty) scales. You can swim ___fast___ (quickly) and ___jump___ (leap) high.

I ___smile___ (grin) every time I see you. You make me ___laugh___ (giggle).

Your ___friend___ (pal),

Frankie

Page 61

4 2 5 4 2
Total centimeters: __17__

4 4 2 2 3
Total centimeters: __15__

2 2 2 2 2 3 3
Total centimeters: __16__

Page 62

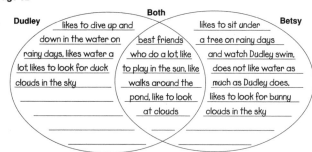

Dudley — likes to dive up and down in the water on rainy days, likes water a lot, likes to look for duck clouds in the sky

Both — best friends who do a lot alike, to play in the sun, like walks around the pond, like to look at clouds

Betsy — likes to sit under a tree on rainy days and watch Dudley swim, does not like water as much as Dudley does, likes to look for bunny clouds in the sky